To: Zayn Kassam

Thank you for your help
on this monograph. See p. 45.

Christian Faith
and Religious Diversity

Lee McDonald
May, 2002

D0001951

FACETS

Christian Faith
and
Religious Diversity

Mobilization for the
Human Family

Edited by
John B. Cobb Jr.

Fortress Press
Minneapolis

CHRISTIAN FAITH AND RELIGIOUS DIVERSITY

Cover and book design: Joseph Bonyata
Cover graphic: Copyright © nonstøck inc.
Used by permission.

0-8006-3483-7

The paper used in this publication meets the minimum requirements of American National Standard for Information Sciences—Permanence of Paper for Printed Library Materials, ANSI Z329.48-1984.

Manufactured in the U.S.A.   AF 1-3483

06   05   04   03   02   1   2   3   4   5   6   7   8   9   10

Preface

The Mobilization for the Human Family was organized in 1995 to give expression to the convictions and commitments of progressive Christians (chiefly Protestants) in the greater Los Angeles area. It has worked with people moving from welfare to work, has led in human rights movements, especially around gay issues, is studying the global system that generates sweatshops and protesting against them, and is working for reform of drug policies and the prison system. Because it believes that a major need of the church is to think theologically about currently important issues, it produces position papers, of which this book is one. The office of the Mobilization is located at 1325 N. College Ave., Claremont, CA 91711. The director, Richard Bunce, can be reached at mobilize@tstonramp.com.

This work is the outgrowth of an unusual number of contributions. Most of them were from members of the Mobilization family. However, we sought and received help in formulating the statements about other religious communities from some who stand in other traditions. We acknowledge with special appreciation the assistance of David Chappell, Zayn Kassam, Michael Kuhlwein, and James A. Nelson.

Re-Thinking Our Faith
in the Context of
Religious Diversity

"I was all set to choose Yoko—she knows the job and she seems like a good person to work with. But I don't see how we could have a Buddhist as the financial secretary of a Methodist Church. The financial secretary has to interact with our members. How would Mrs. Stanhope feel if she knew she was talking to a Buddhist?"

"But you said that Yoko was by far the best qualified of the applicants. Of course our financial secretary needs to work with our members—to respect them and their religion. How does she feel about working in a church?"

"She told me that some of her family are Christians, but that when she began to think for herself, she found more depth and reality in the old tradition of her grandparents. She doesn't seem at all defensive or want to argue about religious differences."

Yoko was hired, and five years later, the church administrator made the following comment: "How good that we chose Yoko. All this time she has kept our accounts perfectly. She says she is an even stronger Buddhist than she was when she came to work for us, but she always has shown respect for our ways too. We have grown to trust each other, not only about money, but about understanding each other too. I think that most of our members have come to respect her kind of faith a lot more than they did at the start."

A Burning Issue

Few questions are more troubling to Christians today than how to understand our faith in relation to the diversity of ways our friends and neighbors think and live. From the Reformation down through the nineteenth century, in the Christian West, the issue of religious diversity was chiefly a matter of the multiple forms of Christianity; and after a period in which Christians fought against and persecuted one another over their differences, they agreed to live and let live. In this country Protestants

developed an understanding of "denominations" as Christian organizations with
particular and distinctive emphases that
recognized one another as equally Christian bodies. Of course, not all Christians
have accepted this solution. There are still
Protestant groups that are far more exclusivist, believing that the rest of us are
committing serious errors that cannot be
tolerated. And while Roman Catholics and
Eastern Orthodox have accepted the role of
being denominations among others for
practical purposes, their official positions
are not this egalitarian. Nevertheless, the
problem in its acute form, both sociologi-
cally and theologically, has been largely
resolved for many Christians. For them
ecumenical dialogue has replaced hostility
or isolation.

Today, the burning issue for Christians in
America, as for Christians in Asia and
Africa, is the relation of Christianity to other
religious communities. We Americans now
live in a much more religiously diverse society. This diversity is especially marked in
California. Since the student body of 17,000
at the Irvine campus of the University of
California is the most culturally diverse in
the system, the school annually holds a

Religious Diversity Faire in which many religious traditions have opportunities to present themselves to the general public in panels, lectures, and demonstrations led by educators and theologians, who are clergy, lay, and Catholic sisters. Events like these heighten awareness that southern Californians live among Protestants, Catholics, Eastern Orthodox, Jews, Muslims, Baha'is, Hindus, Sikhs, Buddhists, Confucians, Taoists, and Native Americans who practice their traditional ways.

The awareness of religious diversity leads some Christians to intensify their view that only through belief in Jesus Christ can anyone be saved. Others assume that this is what a Christian must believe and, for just that reason, distance themselves from the church altogether. We believe that a vital Christian faith calls for positive appreciation of other religious traditions and for rethinking tradition to make this explicit.

This book is divided into two major parts. The first part describes ways in which Christians can respond to this awareness of religious diversity in faithfulness to scripture and tradition without negative teachings about other traditions that have characterized most of our past. The second part offers resources for understanding the richness of the diversity within which we live. It sets this in the context of a history of the increase of religious diversity in the United States. The brief accounts of nine religious communities (other than Christian ones) have been developed in careful interaction with persons who participate in these communities or have strong sympathies toward them. The book concludes with practical proposals of actions that congregations can take to express their appreciative relation to other religious communities.

Transforming Christian Teaching

1. Biblical history

The Jewish scriptures that have been transformed into the Christian Old Testament are not preoccupied with the question of religious diversity. They focus primarily on issues internal to Israel. Here there is a strong emphasis on devotion only to Israel's God and condemnation of any worship of the deities of other peoples. At least by the time of Jeremiah, the prophets were not only opposing the worship of other deities, but also denying their reality. Most emphasized that the one true God worked in and through people who were outside of the Jewish community. Some dreamed of a time when people from all over the world would come to Jerusalem to worship God and learn Torah.

For many Jews the conviction that they alone were worshipping the true God led to an intensification of their devotion and willingness to sacrifice for their faith. The stories of Joseph, David, and Esther encouraged Jews in Diaspora to remain monotheistic. The prophets often spoke of God's working with foreign forces. Jews resisted any interference in their religious observance so fiercely that they won special consideration from their Roman rulers. Some Jews drew the conclusion that they should also seek to convert Gentiles to the Jewish faith. Jesus is quoted as having been sharply critical of Jewish missions of this sort (Matthew 23:15). In any case, many Gentiles were attracted to Jewish synagogues apart from missionary efforts.

Jesus, like most Jewish teachers of his time, addressed himself primarily to other Jews. He had definite views about what God required of them, and he was sharply critical of what he saw as distortions of true Jewish teaching and practice. Under special circumstances, he extended his ministry to Gentiles who asked for his help.

The first communities of followers were Jews. They contested with other Jewish groups, especially the Pharisees, for influence among the Jewish people. This conflict led to strong language by Jesus' followers against their Jewish rivals, condemning them for their refusal to accept Jesus as the Messiah. Exclusivist statements were made implying that those Jews who rejected Jesus could not be saved. Some of this language was attributed to Jesus himself.

The writings that became the Gospels grew, in part, out of these inner-Jewish controversies. Taken out of their context in the struggle of a Jewish sect against more powerful groups of Jews, they have led later generations of Christians to extreme forms of anti-Judaism. This problem of Christian anti-Judaism is so distinctive and so important that it requires separate treatment beyond what can be said in this book. We are hoping to produce a paper on this topic.

At a very early stage in the development of the Jesus movement, the conviction that

Jesus had freed his followers from Jewish ceremonial law led to the removal of the barriers that Judaism in general had placed in the way of Gentile conversions. The greatest barrier had been the requirement of circumcision. The decision that this was not necessary made the Jesus movement attractive to the Gentiles who were already associated in a secondary status with Jewish synagogues dispersed throughout the Roman Empire. It also freed members of the Jesus movement, such as Paul, to express the missionary logic of the belief that the God of Israel was the only true God. Hence, it was in its Christian form that the Jewish heritage spread throughout the Roman Empire, eventually becoming dominant.

Until Christians became politically powerful, the exclusivist teachings found in Christian scriptures were not a major problem. The primary quest of the early Christians had been for freedom to practice their own convictions and to share them with others. But once Christianity gained political power, its exclusivist claim led it to seek the suppression of competing communities. There is much in the ensuing history of which we can only repent.

2. New Testament Texts

Let us look now at some of the texts that have seemed to many Christians to justify the denial of religious value to other traditions and communities. Do these texts imply just the meanings that have typically been drawn from them? If so, must we simply reject these biblical teachings or can we understand them better?

Many of the verses that most disturb us today are from the Gospel of John. Here much is placed on the lips of Jesus that is radically different from what he says in the Synoptics: Matthew, Mark, and Luke. Generations of scholars have argued that few if any of these discourses are actually verbatim expressions of Jesus' own teaching.

That does not mean that Christians should take these teachings lightly. They express the convictions of Christian believers of an early generation. Whether these Christians themselves thought that the historical Jesus spoke in this way, we do not know. But they certainly believed that these sayings were of God.

Perhaps the most difficult passage for those who refuse to condemn all who find life and meaning in other communities is

John 3:17-21. There we are told that "those who do not believe are condemned already." (18) The belief in question is in the Son whom God sent into the world. "The light has come into the world, and people loved darkness rather than light because their deeds were evil" (19).

This verse certainly points to a sharp separation between those who were drawn to the divine light that shone through Jesus and those who refused to acknowledge that light. The context of this saying is the Jewish community in which Jesus lived. The idea can apply directly only to those who actually encountered Jesus. We may feel that it is unfair to the Jews who rejected him during his ministry, but the point is not meaningless in that context. If we share with the author the belief that the light of God was embodied in Jesus with extraordinary clarity and purity, then we can also share the view that how people responded to him expressed something very fundamental about themselves.

In any case, according to this text, those who fail to respond to Jesus are simply left in the darkness and wickedness in which they were already immersed. No further evil is imposed upon them. If there are those who have escaped from that darkness and wickedness by other means, they, too, presumably, would remain in the new condition they have reached. Whatever blessedness they have attained remains theirs, however they have reached it. There is no suggestion that Jesus came to destroy what was good in the world to which he came. Hence, even these seemingly exclusivist verses do not have the meaning the church has too often read into them.

Over the centuries Jesus has been presented to people in more and more diverse forms. In some cases, what it has meant to people to encounter what they understand by "Jesus" has not been good news. If the "Jesus" some encounter is one who demands obedience to the church in order to avoid eternal hellfire, both acceptance and rejection have entirely different meanings from those proffered in the Bible. If other people encounter a "Jesus" who requires them to repudiate a rich tradition of wisdom in order to enter a pietistic and exclusivist community, their refusal does not imply that they "love darkness." On the other side, there are many who are drawn to the Jesus of the Gospels who see no reason to abandon their own communities and join a Christian church. Mohandas Gandhi is the most famous example, but there have been many others.

One way of reading the Gospel is in light of the Prologue. There we learn that the true subject of speech and action in the Gospel is actually the Word (Logos) who became incarnate in Jesus. This Word was with God from the beginning and was, indeed, divine.

If we consider in this light the apparently exclusivist statement placed on the lips of Jesus, "I am the way, the truth, and the life" (John 14:6), the implication is far less disturbing. It is the Word of God that is the way, the truth, and the life as affirmed in the Psalter. (See Psalm 119:105.) Certainly Christians believe that that Word was incarnate in Jesus and that the Word's meaning for us was revealed in him. In the Gospel of John, that meaning is that God loves us and that we should love God and one another. Since the Word who is incarnate in Jesus is also the One through whom all things were made and who enlightens everyone (John 1:3-4), we should expect that divine wisdom is to be found also among those who know nothing of Jesus and who find deep meaning in other traditions.

Many find the conclusion of the verse

still more troubling: "No one comes to the Father except through me." Again, if we understand that the "me" in question is the Word of which we read in the Prologue, we need not see this assertion as denying access to God to all who do not relate primarily to the historical Jesus. Since nothing came into being except through the Word, and since the Word is the light of understanding in all people, it is not surprising that we cannot come to God apart from that Word.

The use of the Christian doctrine of the Word (or Logos) to make the gospel credible to non-believers and to remind believers of truth and wisdom found outside the Christian sphere is not a recent innovation. It was a major factor in the early church, justifying especially the great appreciation of Plato among Christian theologians. In the scholastic theology that culminated in St. Thomas, when arguments were assembled for and against a proposed thesis, Greek and Roman thinkers uninfluenced by Christian scriptures were often cited as authorities alongside Christian theologians and biblical passages. In general the church assumed that God's Wisdom could be found even apart from her incarnation in

Jesus, although its normative embodiment for Christians is always Jesus Christ.

3. The New Testament Understanding of Salvation

Texts that have led Christians to exclusivist conclusions are found in other parts of the New Testament as well (for example, Acts 4:12). Each requires separate treatment. But it may be even more important to consider broader questions about the salvation that is supposed to be exclusive to Christians.

Many suppose that the standard Christian teaching is that of judgment after death, with the saved going to heaven and the damned going to hell. They then understand that Christians teach that the criterion by which this judgment is made is a particular kind of belief in and about Jesus Christ. Accordingly, many suppose that to accept Christianity is to believe that members of all other religious communities are destined for hell. Such people read the exclusivist tendencies of the verses discussed above, as well as others, from this perspective. The resulting revulsion against Christianity is understandable and even admirable. We might say it is truly Christian.

It is important to recognize that this

combination of doctrines is nowhere clearly taught in the New Testament. The passage in the Gospels that speaks most clearly about a final judgment that will divide the saved from the damned is Matthew 25:31-46. Here the criterion for inheriting the realm provided by God has to do with feeding the hungry, giving drink to the thirsty, clothing the naked, caring for the sick, and visiting prisoners. Nothing is said of having faith in Jesus Christ. Nothing in the passage implies that Buddhists or Muslims would be excluded from the realm if they have cared for their neighbors, or that those who identify themselves as believers in Jesus Christ will be rewarded simply for that belief.

Another of the few Gospel passages that speak of final judgment is Luke 16:19-31. Here again belief in Jesus Christ plays no role in the destinies of Lazarus and the rich man. The rich man is punished because he did not heed the law and the prophets. The story goes on to say that people like him will not heed even one who returns from the dead to warn them of the consequences of their actions.

Far more central to Jesus' teaching as presented in the synoptic Gospels is the coming of the realm of God. This is the longed-for situation in which God's will is done on earth as it is in heaven. In the community surrounding Jesus there is already a foretaste of that situation. Also, to be a part of that community is to pray for the coming of this New Age and to live by its values as they reverse the values of this world. But in most of the pronouncements, there is no suggestion that those who fail to believe in Jesus Christ are to be excluded or that God cannot work through those who are not believers in bringing the new situation to pass.

Paul, also, affirms that we are judged in terms of our righteousness. "There will be anguish and distress for everyone who does evil, the Jew first and also the Greek, and honor and peace for everyone who does good, the Jew first and also the Greek" (Romans 2:9). But Paul enriches the picture because of his doubt that when judged by our own righteousness any of us can justify ourselves. Hence he emphasizes the importance of God's grace, a gift that we cannot earn but, instead, receive through faith. Through faith we participate in the righteousness of Jesus Christ. Paul speaks ecstatically about the gifts that come to believers. He does not speak of punishments being meted out to those who do not believe. They are simply left in the sinful and degraded situation into which Paul believes their failure to acknowledge God has brought them.

Obviously, there is no discussion in Paul of how other great spiritual teachers, such as those in India, responded to the human condition. They tended, like Paul, to view it bleakly. Like him, they proposed radical ways of escaping it. To take Paul's enthusiasm for the new way opened up by Jesus Christ as a condemnation of other ways of whose existence he was entirely ignorant is hardly persuasive.

4. Historical Developments

We must acknowledge that the picture of our ultimate destiny as heaven or hell, with this decided by our beliefs, rather than by our relationship to other people, became widespread in the Christian tradition. It led conscientious Christians to engage in strenuous efforts to convert those who did not believe. It often promoted this conversion in some separation from the concern for justice and righteousness. Conscientious Christians have done much evil because of this

set of doctrines. Matters have been even
worse when conversion has been associated
with the expansion of national and imperial
rule. The church's role in the European
invasion and conquest of Latin America is
full of horror stories, beginning with geno-
cide of the natives of the Caribbean islands.
In North America the situation was little
better. Further, the Christianity to which
native peoples were to be converted was
identified with the culture of the converters.
The leadership of Christian churches in the
effort to force Native Americans to assimi-
late into Euro-American culture is an especially ugly chapter in this history. All too
often missions have served, and even now
continue to serve, colonial masters, provid-
ing justification for their greed.

Since in the modern age Europeans and
Euro-Americans carried on most of the missionary work, and since they tended to be
patronizing, at best, and contemptuous, at
worst, toward persons of other ethnicities or
races, modern Christian missions have often
been racist. Indeed, some Christians used
the Bible to justify the enslavement of other
races. Black Africans suffered most from
this perversion of Christianity. Even now,
when there is universal recognition that the

Bible stands against slavery, subtler forms of racism continue to pervade the behavior of predominantly white churches.

Fortunately, there have been other ways of understanding Christianity and other types of missionary activity. None has been perfect, but in an imperfect world, they can be celebrated all the same. For example, one of the great modern Christian missions was to China in the sixteenth and seventeenth centuries. The Jesuits were far from contemptuous of Chinese civilization. They found much in it that they recognized as superior to the European civilization of the time. They thought highly of the Confucian teaching that so richly informed Chinese life. Nevertheless, they believed that they had in Jesus Christ something of great value to offer China. They persuaded many of the leaders of China that this was true. Some converted to Christianity. More were ready to do so if they could be assured that this would not involve abandonment of the Confucian teaching, culture, and way of life on which Chinese governance was based.

The Jesuits agreed with the Chinese that rejection of Confucianism should not be required as a condition of becoming

Christian. But they needed the agreement of the papacy. The papacy vacillated over a long period of time, and the Chinese court finally rejected Christianity in disgust.

Even in missions that were much more closely tied to Western imperialism, there were missionaries who did not separate the gospel from justice. Many supported the causes of colonized people against the colonizers or at least undertook to moderate the exploitation the colonizers inflicted. Furthermore, even if unintentionally, they gave to colonized people a Bible that could empower them in their quest for liberation.

The connection between the gospel and meeting the needs of those to whom it was brought was especially prominent in the missionary movement that came to prominence in the late nineteenth century and caught the imagination of the churches in the first decades of the twentieth. Much of this movement was closely related to the Social Gospel. Here the understanding of the gospel did not have to do with rescuing people from hell but with bringing them into participation in God's realm, where God's will is done. The missionaries taught the gospel of God's loving concern for each individual and for society as a whole and

God's call to believers to share in working for the coming of God's realm. They understood this work to involve education, improving the position of women, health care, agricultural development, democracy, and greater economic justice as well as peace and goodwill among nations. They planted churches that would nurture this whole range of concerns as well as ministering to more personal needs.

Needless to say, there are many valid criticisms of these efforts as well. But they demonstrate that Christians can be motivated by their faith to devote themselves to the overall betterment of others in some independence of whether they accept Christian beliefs. Much of the Christian missionary activity of the old-line American denominations has this character today.

Early in the century, some missionaries developed an appreciative relation to other religious traditions, and in the Second World Missionary Conference, meeting in Jerusalem in 1928, there was talk of a common front of the world's religious communities against the rising power of secularism and atheism. The subsequent rise to dominance of Barthian theology pushed this type of missionary thinking aside for fifty years.

It is, therefore, a mistake to think that past Christian teaching about how we should relate to people belonging to other religious traditions is to be equated with the idea that Christians should rescue the heathen from an eternity in hell by evoking their belief in Christian teaching. To reject that formula today is not to initiate a new type of Christianity but to side with some emphases in the New Testament and the tradition against others. Nevertheless, it would also be a mistake to suppose that we can find in the tradition ready-made answers to the questions that our new, radically pluralistic, situation drives us to ask.

5. Two Widespread Contemporary Responses to Religious Diversity: Exclusivism and Pluralism

Christianity has not been alone among the religious traditions in viewing itself as the one way. The tension between such an exclusivist claim and open appreciation of other traditions is felt in a number of communities today. Some resolve the issue by a measure of indifference as to what happens to other traditions as long as they are themselves left alone to pursue their way. Many Jews and Native Americans respond in this way. Others have a keen interest in sharing their insights and wisdom with others. The United States has been a fertile mission field, especially for Hindus and Buddhists. Happily, their missions have not been tainted with connections to imperialism or colonialism or racism. A third response has been a keen interest in coming to fuller mutual understanding and appreciation of one another through dialogue and cooperation.

We Christians have a valid interest in how members of other communities work out their responses to the pluralistic situation in which we are all engulfed. We may profit from learning how they adapt and adjust, and we may develop ideas that are helpful to them. But as Christians, our primary task is to work out our Christian response, leaving to others the freedom to work out theirs.

Among Christians, it seems, there are two responses that come most easily to mind, and these lead to a sharp polarization among us. Many seem, wrongly, to suppose that these are the only possibilities. They are often called (1) "exclusivism" and (2) "pluralism."

Exclusivism and Its Limitations. Exclusivists hold that whatever positive values other religious traditions have, they do not save their adherents. Only Christian faith is salvific. Similarly, whatever merits other religious leaders or founders may have, they cannot offer the ultimate truth that is given only in Jesus Christ. Exclusivists may affirm that we should be respectful of others and give them religious freedom. They may agree that Christians should repent for much that we have done to others in the past. But they are convinced that this in no way counters the truth that between Christian faith and all other religious activities and attitudes there is a great difference. Only in the former is there ultimate truth and salvation. They believe that to give up the view that Jesus Christ is the one Lord and Savior of all people is to abandon Christian faith itself. The basic stance of Christians toward adherents of other religious traditions, in the exclusivist view, should be to seek their conversion to Christianity. For exclusivists, only this effort adequately expresses Christian love.

Our formulations above express our rejection of this view. We are called to approach other religious communities with full respect for their experience and the affirmations they have been led to make. We should not assume the superiority of our experience and convictions but should be eager to learn from others.

Pluralism and Its Limitations. Many of those with whom we share this position call themselves "pluralists." Christian pluralists do not question the truth and saving value to be found in Christianity, but they see no reason to suppose that Christianity is the *only* path to truth and salvation. Instead they believe that there are multiple ways of attaining salvation, and they often use the image of many paths up the same mountain. What other paths there are is to be learned as we encounter other religious communities and see the positive effects their beliefs and practices have on the lives of their members. Pluralists believe that all religious traditions should be judged by their effectiveness in mediating salvation to their members. They may disagree as to exactly what this salvation consists in, but they share the conviction that there is a common goal toward which all religious traditions are directed.

Christian pluralists usually concede to

exclusivists that there are strong exclusivist tendencies in both scripture and tradition. But they point out that this is true of other religious traditions as well. Today, pluralists are convinced, we are in a position to view all of the religious traditions with more objectivity and detachment. In this perspective, we appreciate the achievements of all, but we see that most have failed to recognize adequately the diversity of paths to salvation. Pluralists call for all religious traditions to give up their exclusivist claims.

We agree with pluralists that all the great religious traditions deserve not only toleration, but also appreciation and respect. Accordingly, we share many of their views about how Christians should relate to the other traditions. First, we must work for a context in which all can flourish. Second, we will seek dialogue to increase mutual understanding wherever others are willing to engage in it. Third, we will seek relations with each tradition individually that express our appropriate connection with that community. Fourth, we will undertake to cooperate with all who are willing to do so on projects for the common good. Fifth, we will undertake to formulate our own teachings in ways that discourage any sense of our own superiority or negative attitudes toward others.

Although we appreciate the commitment of Christian pluralists to the acceptance of other religious traditions as basically equal with our own, we find their position not "pluralistic" enough. It fails to appreciate the depth of differences among the traditions. These differences are not simply in the way they perceive a common goal but also in their conception of the goal itself. Instead of assuming that the several traditions are all different paths up the same mountain, we need to recognize that in some cases they lead up different mountains.

One problem with what we have called "pluralism" above is that it asks each tradition to relativize its affirmations. It rejects the universal claims of all traditions. It supposes that only in this way can believers in one community accept believers in other communities on an equal basis.

The rejection of all universal claims has results that are in deep conflict with our historic beliefs. For example, the relativization of the idea that God loves all people is problematic for Christians. We have always supposed that this is true even for those who do not recognize its truth. To be told that its truth is limited to the Christian community is deeply disturbing and contrary to our understanding of the whole of reality. To think in that way could have quite negative practical consequences.

Furthermore, this rejection of all universal claims is equally disturbing to persons in other religious communities. The relativization of Buddhist teaching, for example, is just as difficult for a Buddhist to accept as the relativization of Christian teaching is for a Christian. Buddhists believe that Buddha-nature characterizes all things whatsoever. They understand that only Buddhists may recognize this, but they do not believe that it is true only for them. To say that Buddha-nature is the true nature of all things only for Buddhists is as troubling to Buddhists as it is troubling for Christians to say that God's love for all is true only for Christians.

A Fuller Pluralism. A deeper appreciation for difference, a more authentic pluralism, is possible. Instead of asking each religious community to relativize its claims, we may find that the universal truth of the claims of one tradition is not in contradiction with the universal truth of the claims of another tradition. Perhaps Buddhists are correct that all creatures are instances of Buddha-nature. This can be explained in language that does not entail the word "Buddha." Indeed, it is often formulated in terms of "emptiness" or "dependent origination." The point is that all things are imperma-nent and insubstantial. Nothing exists independently. Each thing or event comes into being out of the conjunction of other things and participates in the coming to be of other things. The Buddhist goes on to say that when we recognize this about all things, and especially about our selves, we experience the world as it truly is and are freed from the illusions that bind us to it. We can live in true freedom, wise and com-passionate.

One may agree or disagree with Bud-dhists about the nature of reality. But there is nothing in these universal claims that conflicts with the Christian claim that God loves all persons. Buddhists may not believe this, but their failure to believe is not caused by their affirmation of the uni-versality of Buddha-nature unless Chris-tians formulate belief in God in a way that contradicts this Buddhist teaching. Chris-tians need not do this. Hence, in principle, the universal claims of both Buddhism and Christianity may be true. Rather than relativizing both, and thereby denying the truth of the deepest convictions of both Buddhists and Christians, one may affirm both. One may affirm both, not because they are two ways of saying the same thing, or because they point to two ways of attaining the same end, but because they are answers to different questions and suggest different goals for human life.

This way of dealing with the otherness of Buddhism does not work well with Islam. In this relation we must recognize far more similarities. Allah is the Muslim name for the God of the Bible. There are many ways of understanding Allah among Muslims, and there are many ways of understanding God among Christians, but all of these are ways of understanding the God of Israel; and these Muslim and Christian ways of understanding overlap extensively. Muhammad was very much aware of Christianity, and he was, in many ways, respectful toward it. We worship the same God.

In some ways that makes our relations with Islam more difficult than our relations with Buddhism. Muhammad gave high honor to Jesus, affirming, for example, his virgin birth. But he rejected the doctrines of incarnation and Trinity. These have often been the points of chief dispute between the two traditions. The pluralists we have discussed above can argue that these doctrines work for Christians but have no universal truth, but this is not a satisfactory solution.

Many Christians today, however, would share Muhammad's rejection of the doctrine of the Trinity as he understood it. He thought that the doctrine of Trinity denied the unity of God, and he shared with Jews a strong commitment to that unity. In fact, however, classic explanations of the Trinity, especially in the West, insist that the unity of the three persons of the Trinity is to be preserved. One may question the success of some of these formulations in adequately preserving the unity, but the intention is not at odds with Islamic concerns. Christians believe in one God, not three Gods. Muslims (like Jews) also recognize that there are many names for God, highlighting different aspects of the way God relates to the world.

In relation to Islam, the great need is for Christians to develop a far more positive appreciation of Muhammad's prophetic role and of the teaching of the Qur'an, as for example its deep concern for the poor and its toleration of Jews and Christians. The Qur'an is generous in its appraisal of Jesus. Christians on the whole have not been generous in our appraisal of Muhammad and the Qur'an. For this we should repent.

Such repentance will not lead to total agreement. For example, there are teachings about the death of Jesus in the Qur'an that Christians cannot accept; and there are Christian teachings about the death and resurrection of Jesus that Muslims reject. But friendly argument in the context of mutual respect is not to be avoided. Many Christians, however, may find more agreement with many Muslims than they do with some fellow Christians. In the context of encounter and conversation, Christians are likely to be deeply impressed by the continuing success of Islam in shaping the whole lives of believers and in resisting features of modernity that are in conflict with the teachings of both traditions.

This is not the place to discuss the stance of Christians toward each of the other religious traditions separately. Enough has been said to indicate that sweeping statements about "other religions" are unlikely to be accurate or helpful. Each religious tradition should be approached on its own distinct terms. The accounts of nine religious communities present in the United States, offered in "Our Pluralistic Context" (p. 37), provides a basis for considering how each is best approached by Christians.

6. A Third Contemporary Approach: The Transformation of Christian Teaching

Clearly, we must transform our teachings. In their dominant formulation in the past they have been negative toward other religious traditions. They must be reformulated so as to help Christians to understand that, precisely out of the depth of our faith, we are called to love and listen to others with admiration and appreciation for their lives and their insights. Rather than thinking that the acceptance of other traditions as equal partners in our society is a compromise, we must learn to see it as an expression of our faith in Christ.

The most urgent transformation of all is already taking place. Traditional Christian teaching has vilified Jews and Judaism. This has resulted in an appalling history of pogroms and other forms of persecution culminating in the Holocaust. All Christians share responsibility for this evil, and all Christian teaching must be carefully reformulated so as, at a minimum, to avoid arousing animosity toward Jews. Positively we need to go beyond this to cultivate in Christians a deep appreciation not only for our debt to ancient Jews but also to contemporary Judaism.

In order to make the changes we need not only in our teaching about Judaism but also in our general teaching, we must overcome the Christian tendency to suppose that all the truth we require is already given to us from our Christian past. This idolatry of our heritage is repudiated within that heritage. The New Testament itself points us to the future. Paul writes: "Now we see in a mirror dimly, but then we will see face to face" (1 Cor. 13:12). According to John, Jesus promised to send us the Spirit of truth who will guide us into all the truth (John 16:12). More fundamentally, Jesus taught us to pray for the coming of the realm of God in which God's purposes will be fulfilled. We live toward that future, not with all the knowledge and understanding that we need, but with openness to learning from others and working with others toward that end.

There is nothing new about learning from others. The Bible itself reflects a long history of the transmission and transformation of traditions. The beliefs expressed in the pre-exilic period differ from post-exilic ones. There is growth toward greater universality. Scholars trace the influence of Sumerian, Egyptian, Canaanite, Babylonian, Persian, and Greek ideas and culture in the history of Israel. This does not mean that the faith of Israel was syncretistic, but it does mean that Israel learned from and was repeatedly transformed by the cultural and religious achievements of other peoples.

This process continued in Christianity. There is profound Hellenistic influence in the New Testament. As Christianity became more and more Gentile in its membership, Greek culture played an ever-larger role. The great thinkers of the early church incorporated much of Neo-Platonic thought in their formulations of Christian theology. Aristotelian philosophy became a dominant factor in the medieval period. In general, Christians both supported the rise of natural science and also adapted their theology to what they learned from it. In the past two centuries Christians have led in historical study, including study of our own history, and many have adapted our teaching to what has been learned there. Much the same can be said of the social and psychological sciences. In short, much of Christianity has been in a continuous process of transformation through its encounter with new forms of wisdom and knowledge.

Needless to say, this process has often been controversial and has included many mistakes. Christians have needed to discriminate among the many claims for our belief, and sometimes we have failed to do this well. We have sometimes rejected what we should have accepted and accepted what we should have rejected. Later generations have had to purify the faith from cultural accretions that have distorted it. For example, we suffer now from some of the effects of Hellenization, and also from too uncritical an acceptance of the scientific worldview. But openness to learning from Greek philosophy and from the sciences has been crucial to the survival and growth of Christianity.

We now face a great new opportunity. Whereas in the past within the West the privilege of learning from the wisdom of indigenous people and from the traditions of South and East Asia was limited to a few scholars, now it is available to masses. A Christian faith that, for good and evil, was indigenized primarily in a Hellenistic culture is encountering the religious traditions of India and China and discovering the great wisdom of indigenous people. It can gain in this encounter just as much as it gained earlier from Hellenism and science. If it does so, it will be as deeply transformed.

Our Pluralistic Context

Progressive Christians, while being conscious of the great diversity of religious groups in the United States and the world, as yet have no national consensus on the best policies for living amicably in a religiously pluralistic society. This book includes outlines of nine other religious faiths: Judaism, Islam, Baha'i, Hinduism, Sikhism, Buddhism, Confucianism, Taoism, Native American Religion. How we relate to and understand them is important to our progressive Christian faith.

1. American History:
How Our Religious Diversity Arose

Living with religious pluralism implies acceptance of religious freedom. Turning to history, we find the background of the modern concept of religious freedom in the ideas of religious toleration in seventeenth-century England and eighteenth-century America. The idea that there should be freedom of worship for different sects was at that time by no means generally accepted. Indeed, many people regarded it as an outrageous idea, to be rejected by all right-thinking people. Why should government protect the propagation of false doctrine? Others, like John Milton and John Locke in England and Roger Williams and William Penn in America, believed otherwise. In principle, if not always in practice, they thought most persons could be trusted to come to their own conclusions on political and religious matters. Hence they advocated freedom of speech, of the press, and of religious worship. Of these, Roger Williams was probably the most consistent in matching theory with practice. The fear of a Catholic monarchy affected the limits of Milton's and Locke's principles of toleration. In any case, little thought was given to freedom of religion for African slaves.

In a later generation Thomas Jefferson defended a "wall of separation" between church and state, and James Madison persuaded his fellow Congressmen to adopt the Bill of Rights. The First Amendment states: "Congress shall make no law respecting an establishment of religion, or prohibiting the free exercise thereof; or abridging the freedom of speech, or of the press, or the right of the people peaceably to assemble, and to petition the Government for a redress of grievances." It is important to note that this was originally a restriction on federal power alone. Several states had established churches. Virginia, for example, used tax monies to support the Anglican Church. The free speech clause of the First Amendment was not applied to the states until the 1920s and the religion clauses not until the 1940s. Since then, the fine line between protecting free worship and not "establishing" religion has been trod in many contentious court decisions. For example, some church child-care programs have been held to be exempt from taxation, but some have not. Using federal funds for busing students to parochial schools is legal, but buying books for them is not.

In 1800 America was a Protestant culture with small minorities of Catholics and Jews. In addition to these groups, there were several hundred thousand Native Americans, some of whom had been touched by Protestant and Catholic missions, but most of whom preserved strong Native American religious traditions. By 1900, white America displayed a three-way religious pluralism of Protestant, Catholic, and Jew. Alongside these, because of segregation, African Americans had established their own churches, which were primarily Protestant but included Catholics as well as Jews of the Ethiopian tradition.

How did the transformation of white America take place? The answer is found in the waves of immigration, which in the nineteenth century brought to our shores large numbers of both Jews and Catholics. Jewish immigration was stimulated by the reactionary Congress of Vienna (1815) and the failure of the revolutions of 1848. Large numbers of Jews sought the greater freedom of the new world. Initially these immigrants came from Germany and therefore brought with them distinctive forms of German Reform Judaism, stressing the prophetic emphases of the Bible. Its leader in America was Isaac Meyer Wise (1819–1900), rabbi of congregations in Albany, New York, and Cincinnati, and the founder of Hebrew Union College. Later in the nineteenth century some Jewish leaders veered away from what they thought to be the extremes of Reform Judaism, and founded, in 1876, Conservative Judaism, which in doctrine lay between the Reform and Orthodox versions. When the source of immigration shifted from Germany to Poland and Russia, Orthodox Judaism also made its appearance in America.

Catholics had their own reasons for immigrating to America. As a colony, Maryland had been populated early with Catholics, and the Irish potato famine of the 1850s gave Irish families the harsh alternative of migrating or starving. The Catholic bishops, hoping to maintain a vigorous Catholic presence in Protestant America, favored established religion.

None of these developments took place smoothly or easily. The nativist Know-Nothing movement of the 1850s opposed immigration and pushed virulent anti-Catholic measures. The Ku Klux Klan had as its primary purpose terrorizing African Americans so as to keep them in subjection; but in both its nineteenth-century version and its 1920s revival, it judged both Catholics and Jews to be "un-American." By World War II, however, America was well established as a country of Protestants, Catholics, and Jews, divided between Euro-American and segregated African American communities.

After World War II, another pluralism was beginning to assume its distinctive shape. Like the first pluralism, it was driven by immigration, this time largely from Asia and Latin America, as families saw the United States as the "land of the free" and a source of higher income. But there were deep differences as well. The first pluralism claimed a common biblical source; the second could make no such claim. The first had three parties; the second more than doubled this number.

Among the many religious traditions that are now represented in southern California and the nation, we have selected nine. Of these, the first eight entered primarily through immigration, although in several cases they have also won many converts. These eight are Judaism, Islam, Baha'i, Hinduism, Sikhism, Buddhism, Confucianism, and Taoism. The religious traditions of Native Americans have survived the onslaught of Euro-Americans and are today enjoying a certain revival.

2. Nine Religious Groups

Judaism. While Judaism is a party to the first and older American pluralism, it also demands inclusion as a part of the current pluralism. Judaism is, along with Christianity and Islam, a monotheistic religion. Unlike them it is not built on one founder but on a long tradition. It claims to go back to Abraham and Moses, through a line that includes the prophets and the sages of Israel. Abraham is sometimes called the "father of the Hebrew people" and Moses the "law-giver," but the sense of being an historical and uniquely chosen people is crucial.

Early Judaism arose out of the ashes of the Solomonic Temple destroyed by the Babylonians in the sixth-century B.C.E., while Rabbinic Judaism arose out of the ashes of the Second or Herodian Temple destroyed by the Romans in 70 of the Common Era. [Judaism, like other religious traditions has its system of historical dating.

Because the Christian system of Before Christ (B.C.) and Anno Domini (A.D.) is so well established, and since no other system would be more neutral among religious traditions, many who want to overcome triumphalistic Christian rhetoric now propose that we retain use of the familiar dates but describe them differently—as Before the Common Era (B.C.E.) and Common Era (C.E.)]. Early Judaism was a highly diverse religion out of which Christianity and Rabbinic Judaism, along with the much smaller Samaritan religion, were the sole survivors.

While Judaism shares belief in one God and also shares extensive parts of the Bible with Christians, it differs from Christianity in two basic respects: First, whereas Christianity approaches God through faith in Christ, Judaism approaches the same God by practice of Torah, or law, the gift of God to his chosen people. Second, if Christians are asked to explain or interpret faith in Christ, their reply is apt to be in terms of creed and theology. Analogously, asked to explain Torah, Jews reply with Talmud, the body of rabbinical literature that interprets the Bible. The heart of Judaism in all of its forms is Torah, the precious gift of God that distinguished Israel from all other peoples.

"Judaism is Torah and Torah is Judaism."

Torah includes not the Pentateuch alone, but all of the Hebrew Bible and the whole tradition that arises from it, especially the Talmud. Torah is made up of two major components, *halachah,* or law, and *haggadah,* or story. Though neither excludes the other as unimportant, Christianity as an heir of Early Judaism focuses on Torah as *haggadah.*

Rabbinic Judaism since the *Judische Wissenschaft* (Jewish Enlightenment) movement in nineteenth-century Germany has three main branches: Reform Judaism, which adapted Judaism to the concepts of the European Enlightenment, with its many secular and pro-scientific elements; Conservative Judaism, which believed this accommodation had gone too far and reacted against the Enlightenment; and Orthodox Judaism, which to varying degrees consciously resisted and resists accommodation.

Islam. The adherents of the religion of Islam consider themselves to be recipients of the self-same stream of divine guidance granted to Jews and Christians. Indeed, the term "Mohammedanism" is a misnomer, since

Muhammad is not an object of worship; only God can be such. Islam means "submission" to God (Allah). Abraham is commended in the Qur'an (the scripture of the Muslims, also spelled Koran) as having been a Muslim, that is, the first to submit to the divine will, and is considered the common progenitor of the Jews, Christians, and Muslims. As the Sufis or mystics of Islam suggest, prophets among humans are like rubies among rocks; both are stones, but how much more exalted in the beauty of their inner light are prophets. By their proximity to human experience prophets are best able to communicate knowledge about the divine and give instructions from the divine to humans. Thus, while the Qur'an faults Jews in the days of Moses and Aaron for having lapsed into error from the worship of God, and Christians for elevating Jesus Christ into divine status, it nonetheless promises that heaven will be open to the righteous among them. The divine being alone is to be worshipped and acknowledged as the Merciful and Compassionate Creator, while humans are exhorted to live an ethical and spiritual life mindful of being held accountable for social relations in this world and in preparation for a beatific life in the hereafter.

Historically, Islam as a distinct religion began with the divine revelations communicated to Muhammad in the seventh century of the Common Era, revelations that have been collected in the Qur'an. Conversion to Islam was not, as is commonly supposed, due so much to the threat of the sword as to the persuasiveness of preachers, and, at times, to political or economic pressures. Differences over the question of authority and over how the Qur'an is to be understood and applied led within the first two centuries to two communities: the Sunni—those who followed the "custom" of the Prophet, and the Shiah -those who held that leadership for the community had passed on to Ali, Muhammad's cousin and son-in-law. The Sunni hold the five pillars of Islam to be confession, prayer to Allah, tithing, fasting during Ramadan, and pilgrimage to Mecca. Shiah believe that the first three caliphs (successors to Mohammed) were invalid, the first valid caliph being Ali.

The mystical movement in Islam is the Sufi movement. The Sufis add an attitude of spontaneity to the rigorous historical outlook of the Sunnis. References to Islamic *jihad* have often been misunderstood in the West. The assumption is that it refers to violent activity, as in "holy war," whereas in fact its meaning is closer to the English word "crusade," which can be, but need not be, violent. Sufis seek an inward *jihad* against selfishness.

In the United States a new Muslim movement originated in 1930 among African Americans, sometimes called the Nation of Islam. Its adherents are often called Black Muslims, and its early teaching demonized whites as a result of the way in which whites dehumanized African Americans. Under the influence of the historical Islamic teaching and the impact of Martin Luther King Jr. and subsequently Malcolm X, it has de-emphasized its racial component and has increasingly become a recognized part of the larger tradition.

Baha'i. The Baha'i faith was founded in Persia (today's Iran) in the nineteenth century. It is an outgrowth of the Bábi faith and was founded in 1844 by 'Ali Muhammad of Shiraz (1791–1850), who claimed to fulfill the promise of Islam, was persecuted, and put to death. His successor was prophet Husayn 'Ali of Nur (1817–1892), who took the name Bahá'u'lláh in 1863 and died in exile imposed by the Persian and Ottoman governments. His extensive writings form the basis of Baha'i study, but Baha'i worship includes prayers and readings from other religions. The name Baha'i means "follower of glory." The faith emphasizes the oneness of God, the unity of all religions, and the unity of humankind.

Baha'is believe that God provides Messengers at various periods of history to sustain an evolving faith and to serve an ever more complex society. Their faith holds that the ancient and eternal message of God becomes corrupted over time much as a river becomes contaminated as it moves downstream from the source, and the prophets are like filters which remove contamination from the message while adding necessary instruction to cope with changing human circumstances. As humankind evolves and becomes a more mature species, it needs additional guidance appropriate to its development to better understand and apply the eternal truth. Much as teachers instruct a child according to the child's increased understanding as she ages, so do prophets deliver God's message in ways that are appropriate for each age of humankind. Baha'is hold that among the prophets who perform this function are Abraham, Moses, Zoroaster, Buddha, Jesus, Mohammed, and others. Bahá'u'lláh is the most recent of these prophets.

Baha'i followers stress a harmony between science and religion, racial and gender equality, the independent search for truth, avoidance of the extremes of wealth and poverty, universal compulsory education, and the aims of social justice and world peace. There is no clergy. There are seven million Baha'is in the world and about 250,000 in the United States. The American headquarters is in Wilmette, Illinois, where the Baha'i Temple, begun in 1912, is located. Being both open and inclusive of other traditions, the religion tends to have a broad range of adherents, from cosmopolitan intellectuals to rural minorities. Most of the Baha'is are found in developing countries. Europe and America are experiencing a growth in the number of Baha'is.

Hinduism. The term "Hinduism" is a Western-originated word, derived from the Sanskrit *sindhu* or "river," for the central tradition of Indian religion. To Western observers it appears as infinitely diverse, or multi-verse, the only common trait among its 800 million adherents being the caste system and the inspiration of the Vedas, the ancient collections of religious writings. Two traditions stand out prominently: (1) Vedanta, which combines an acceptance of India's polytheism with a belief in Brahman, which is the Unity or One beyond all variety; and (2) devotional theism of various divinities, notably Krishna, and his holy scripture, the *Bhagavad Gita*. Krishna and Rama are worshipped as savior deities. They are two of the ten *avatars* of Vishnu, the god of preservation, who, with Siva, the god of destruction, form the two primary gods of Hinduism. The paths to spiritual liberation (*Moksha*) are as varied as the psychological types of personality. But, basically, these have been systematized as the Way of the Intellect (*Jnana Marga*), the Way of the Activist (*Karma Marga*), and the Way of the Loving Heart (*Bhakti Marga*). The Way of the Intellect stresses that the ultimate idea is the union of the soul and God, or the surrender of life to Life. The Way of the Loving Heart always retains God as a separate divine Person who can be worshipped.

While Hinduism served its followers well for many centuries, it had to change in order to cope with the altered situation brought about by colonialism, urbanization, and the work of Christian missions. Therefore it experienced a kind of revival in the nineteenth and twentieth centuries, as evinced by such leaders as Vivekananda (1853–1902), Tagore (1861–1941), Aurobindo (1872– 950), and Gandhi (1869–1948).

Today Hinduism shows remarkable vitality. Not only has it gained this vitality in India and among Indian immigrants to the United States, but it also has had extensive influence among Euro-Americans. Yogic disciplines are practiced by millions as a means to an integral health and wholeness of body, mind, and spirit. In addition, Vedantic missionaries have convinced many intellectuals that the deepest insight is common to the mystics of all religious traditions: namely, the identity of one's underlying and truly authentic self (*Atman*) and the ultimate underlying reality (*Brahman*). The most advanced Yogic disciplines are the means of spiritually and existentially realizing this identity.

Sikhism. The word *sikh* means "disciple" in the Punjabi language of north India, and Sikhs are considered "seekers of truth." Sikhism was founded by Guru Nanak (1469–1530) at a time when militarily victorious Muslims were aggressively converting Hindus. Nanak, who was originally a Hindu, traveled throughout India and the Near East accompanied by one Muslim and one Hindu musician, singing praise to God. His primary message was that there exists one God, called by many different names. He taught that one should meditate on God and be supportive of others who did likewise, even though their forms of worship might be different. He believed in the equality of all people, and advocated an end to the Indian caste system and inter-religious strife.

After Nanak, there was a succession of nine more Gurus. The ten Gurus represent ten divine attributes: humility, obedience, equality, service, self-sacrifice, justice, mercy, purity, tranquility, and royal courage. Some of these men developed a military tradition, and Sikhism came to be known as the Path of the Soldier Saint. (A Sikh has often been India's Minister of Defense.) The fifth Guru, Arjun, sent out a call for poetry written by anyone on divine union with the infinite Lord. He collected verses written by mystics from many different religious traditions and called these scriptures Siri Guru Granth Sahib. The tenth and last Guru, Gobind Singh (1666–1708), stated that the form of Sikhism had been set in these scriptures, that they were a living consciousness of the Guru.

According to these scriptures, all of Sikhism is focused on the direct experience of God. Sikh practice is explained in a fourfold way—*Bana:* the physical form (for example, leaving hair uncut, as created by God, avoiding meat and intoxicants); *Bani:* the word of God directly expressed in the scriptures; *Seva:* selfless service; and *Simram:* meditation on God. The spiritual brotherhood and sisterhood of Sikhs is called the Khalsa.

In India the approximately twelve million Sikhs have spread from their native Punjab to all parts of the Indian subcontinent, where they are conspicuous by their beards and turbans. Some Sikhs, mainly as professional people, have found their way to America and England.

Buddhism. Like Christianity, Buddhism is a personally founded religion. Siddhartha Gautama (550–480 B.C.E.) was probably the greatest philosophic mind of classical Indian history. While Jesus has been called Messiah or Christ, Siddhartha has been called the Buddha, often translated as "the Enlightened One," but more accurately "the Awakened One." If we ask from what sleep to what awakening state he arose, he and his followers reply: from the sleep of *samsara* to the awakening of *nirvana*, roughly translated from the false belief that the world of appearance is substantial, to the realization that there is no substantial reality whatsoever. This means that, as opposed to Hindu teaching, there is no underlying self (*Atman*) or ultimate reality (*Bahman*). Enlightenment is the blessed peace at which practitioners arrive when they realize the insubstantial nature of all things and therefore let go of all attachments.

Buddhism shares with Hinduism the idea that all living things are reborn in new lives, or reincarnation. This idea of causation and rebirth is called *karma*. Buddhism teaches a simplified practical form of life in which responsibility for life is the chief cornerstone.

Common to different sects of Buddhism are the "Four Noble Truths" relating to suffering, and the "Eightfold Path" for overcoming suffering. The central ceremony that unifies Buddhists is relying on or taking refuge in the "Three Jewels": namely, the Buddha, his teaching (*dharma*), and the community (*sangha*).

The teaching and community have endured in two major forms: the Theravada tradition using texts written in Pali that thrives in places like Sri Lanka, Burma, and Thailand; and the Mahayana traditions of China, Korea, Japan, and Tibet that use scriptures written in Chinese and Tibetan. Mahayana added many new scriptures to the basic core surviving in Pali, and embodied many new practices. These new departures were encouraged by the idea that exercising wisdom and compassion required creating skillful methods to help others. A new religious model arose called the *bodhisattva* to embody wisdom and compassion, and great *bodhisattva* figures became new objects of worship in Mahayana.

Although Buddhism lacked any central organization except that imposed by state governments, the monastic clergy provided a unifying discipline recognized by both Theravada and Mahayana. In Japan, however, new sects like Pure Land, Nichiren, and Zen allow married clergy; and new lay forms of Buddhism have recently emerged in many Buddhist cultures. In the United States there are many Buddhists who have come from various Asian countries, and there are also many Euro-American converts.

Confucianism. This system of life and thought is not so much a religious tradition as a distinctive humanism. Its Chinese character (*Zen*) represents two humans, symbolizing an ethical relationship, but held under heaven (*t'ien*). Confucius (or Chung Ni, as the Chinese know him) (550–479 B.C.E.) made no claim to divinity or supernatural knowledge. Honor to one's ancestors as a continuing presence in human life has always marked East Asian spirituality. Respect for ancestors and superiors was subsumed into a hierarchy of social and ritual obligations known as *ru-jiao*, the teachings of the scholar-officials, which became the state religion for East Asia. Since the government adopted Confucius as the model sage embodying these virtues, the system became known in the West as Confucianism. Legitimated by heaven, and emphasizing group welfare more than the individual, harmony over justice, and loyalty over personal happiness, Confucianism has created social stability and cultural values that challenge Western individualism.

The idea of an afterlife exists in the Confucian code, but it is not clearly defined.

Confucius propounded the Golden Rule, offered advice to rulers, and delineated social obligations. The qualities of Confucianism, often in combination with other aspects of Chinese tradition, have influenced East Asian religions, including Christianity.

Taoism. Whereas Confucianism sanctifies the social structure, Taoism represents various alternative sources of empowerment beyond that structure. Among its many forms, Taoism includes a counter-cultural tradition flowing from two books, Lao-tzu and Chuang-tzu, that advocate abandoning social conventions as corrupting and instead returning to the way of nature (*Tao*). Against social sophistication, it emphasized intuition, primitivism, meditation, and simplicity by trusting the natural rhythms of things. On the other hand, beginning in 142 C.E., a Heavenly Masters community arose based on revelations from Lao-tzu to a chosen priesthood who were instructed how to command the gods. The Heavenly Master priesthood offered a superior way to save ancestors through repentance and worship that has endured as a liturgical alternative to the imperial cult.

As a result, Taoism prepared for the coming of Buddhism to East Asia, but in turn adopted Buddhist rituals and ideas of *karma* and universal salvation, while influencing Buddhism to produce Zen. Taoism is a radical simplification of life, which always tends toward complexity, superficiality, and confusion. It is a way of being open, honest, and spontaneous and in a delicate harmony with the Creative. The name for this is not important. In fact, it could easily be called the Nameless. But this life or energy produces a rich fruit for living and works especially in lowly and humble ways. This is living in harmony with the

Tao ("the way"). To be "a person of the *Tao*" is the highest calling and the greatest fulfillment. But becoming available to the *Tao* is never easy. It is a life-long process and goes counter to the spirit of any age and its cultural accretions.

Native American Religions. Despite significant variations among 500 tribes and difficulties in distinguishing the older traditions from accommodations to European influence, some generalizations about Native American religions are possible: (1) Stories of creation describe the emergence of the people, suggesting where they should live, declaring the seamless unity of all creation, and calling for profound respect for the Earth and all her creatures. Everything is alive. People are a part of the Earth. Although the Creator sets aside land for their use, they are not owners. At their best, they use only what they need. (2) Harmony is a major belief and value of most Indian people. The creation is harmonious, and all work to maintain, or to restore, harmony with creation and with the community. (3) Most native people have a deep awareness of the spirits of the land and seek to be guided by them in caring for the community. They speak of the Creator as "great Spirit" and "great Mystery," and have no need to explain further. (4) They hold together that which many others separate: spirit/matter, nature/history, cognition/affect, religion/politics/culture, etc. They are intuitive, with their interior reflecting the created world. (5) The community is central to the rituals and ceremonies as well as daily life. Leadership is judged by its ability to serve the people; the economy is organized to feed, shelter, and house all the people. Although the vision quest of the Sioux is solitary, it is in the context of a caring and supportive community. (6) Native peoples are oriented to space rather than to time. They have holy places, not holy weeks or seasons. Nevertheless, while some tribes did not have verb tenses that indicated past or future, they often had a sense of what the Greeks called *kairos*. There were seasons for hunting or farming; there were passages in the life of an individual that marked important transitions.

Practical Implications

Our first part acknowledged that Christians have often made claims of superiority and even of exclusive possession of the way to salvation that have done great harm. We have blinded ourselves to the wisdom of other communities and have often used political, economic, and military power over them abusively. We have much of which to repent.

In the first part we described how our nation has become factually pluralistic so that traditions that we once viewed as remote and irrelevant have come alive in our own neighborhoods. This gives us the chance to change both our thinking and our practice in relation to these communities. We included brief accounts of these traditions that show both their diversity and their respective strengths.

It is time now to consider some practical implications for how we can relate individually and as congregations to these other communities. Few Christians can become richly acquainted with all the other religious communities, even those that are represented in their communities. But most Christians can extend their circles of acquaintance to some degree beyond their Christian neighbors. We can do so with the attitude of respect. We can approach others, hoping to learn not only so as to inform ourselves about their beliefs, customs, and practices but also for the sake of gaining insights and wisdom that can enrich our lives personally and communally.

We Christians are committed, in the words of the World Council of Churches, to peace, justice, and the integrity of creation. As we find others that share these concerns, we can support new interfaith organizations that express and implement our hopes. Whether those should replace our Councils of Churches or supplement them is a practical issue to be considered in each case. But to be genuinely neighborly today must mean establishing positive relations with religious communities other than Christian.

The Presbyterian Church in Claremont, Calif., has for many years been yoked with a Jewish synagogue. Jews and Presbyterians have come to understand and trust one another through annual weeks of exchange visits. At times they extend practical help to one another. This kind of pairing leads to far deeper relations than occasional visits.

There are now a good many interfaith discussion groups in local communities as well as at national and international levels. Through participation in such groups people can come to understand one another and learn from one another. Gradually this affects the congregations from which they come.

This dialogical process does not usually weaken the faith of those who participate. On the contrary, Christians often become more aware of how deeply they are informed by their distinctive faith and come to prize it more. But part of what they come to prize is the encouragement it gives them to open themselves in love to others.

What about evangelism? In relation to vast numbers of people both within and outside the church, communicating the Good News of Jesus Christ is of utmost urgency. This is not the question here.

The question is about evangelism in relating to persons of other faiths. Should we share the Good News that is so important to us with them as well? Before we do so we should consider the reality of the situation in which we relate to them. Many of our neighbors in other religious communities have historical, and even personal, memories of aggressive and even oppressive Christians. They are likely to enter into dialogue with us somewhat hesitantly, fearing that this is just another avenue for us to attempt to convert them. If we use the dialogue for that purpose, we will confirm their fears and drive them away. Similarly, if at the same time that we dialogue we engage in separate evangelistic efforts, they will not trust us.

Given our history, dialogue requires that we create a climate in which there is no manipulation, no effort on anyone's part to convert the others. Christians, especially, need to listen. On the whole, the others know us better than we know them. Much that they know of us renders them distrustful. Our task is to come to understand this distrust, repent of what has engendered it, and work toward a new basis for good relations.

In addition to dialogue, we need to work together on common concerns of community building and social justice. Even when we differ quite markedly in our beliefs, we often find that we share a concern for the relief of human suffering and for maintaining a habitable Earth. Issues of this sort are of such importance that we need to work together with all who are committed to dealing with them.

But none of this means that dialogue precludes honest and open testimony to what we find to be true and important. Quite the contrary. Authentic dialogue requires that we explain our deepest convictions to others even if they are offensive to some of our dialogue partners. We have heard the Good News and been formed by it. We find God in and through Jesus. It is just this that we need to explain to our neighbors of other faiths. With sincerity, conviction, and honesty, our witness to what we believe God has done in Jesus Christ and in the Christian church should be bold and eloquent. In the long run, while we gain wisdom from others, it is our hope that they gain wisdom from us as well.

There are ongoing dialogues in which relationships are established such that people of differing communities are free to try to persuade one another of the truth and value of their beliefs and practices for all. In these dialogues people are free also to criticize one another, pointing out what is offensive to each in the other's tradition. At that point Christians can engage, quite unqualifiedly, in evangelism. By then it is clear that asking others to respond to the Good News of Jesus Christ is not asking them to abandon the wisdom and goodness of their own traditions and cultures.

One urgent issue that few of our churches have addressed is that of interfaith marriage. In an interfaith marriage, a couple has four choices: (1) they can agree to be nonreligious; (2) one spouse can convert; (3) they can celebrate everything and leave the choice to the children at a later date; or (4) they can forge an understanding that binds their religions together while continuing to celebrate both traditions in their distinctiveness. If the couple chooses the first option, it is difficult for the church to help. However, the church should be sensitive to the issues involved in the other three.

The second option is the simplest both for the couple and for the children. It avoids raising the issue of dual faiths within the family. On the other hand, sometimes the one who converts misses what has been left behind and never feels fully at home in the new faith.

The third option provides a more complex spiritual life for the family. However, at some point children are under pressure to choose one or the other, and sometimes this wounds the parent whose faith is abandoned.

The fourth option is the one that this book tends to support most strongly if the couple is capable of the difficult work involved. Within it, both parents can feel spiritually whole and raise spiritually whole children. To achieve this, both must learn the religious and cultural nuances of the other.

In the case of a Christian-Jewish marriage, one of the most important things to understand is that Judaism is practiced primarily in the home, whereas Christianity is practiced outside the home in a church community. To balance the power of Jewish home traditions, Christians may need to develop Christian rituals for home use. Couples should not try to mix traditions in a way that could infringe on the integrity of either. Instead they need to reflect on how both ceremonies can be appreciated as complementary.

Churches can help by having services in which those of other faiths can participate without feeling marginalized or pressured. They can provide contexts in which couples can discuss their struggles and support them in a variety of solutions.

Questions for Discussion

1. What have you learned about other religious communities that interests you?

2. Does understanding the history of religion affect how you understand your own faith? How?

3. What experiences have you had with persons of other faiths?

4. How does the discussion of exclusivists and pluralists relate to your faith? Do you adopt one of these alternatives or reject both?

5. Does this book succeed in making the case for the transformation of Christianity through learning from other traditions?

6. Is Christianity richer and wiser because of the religious diversity of our society?

7. Can we celebrate religious diversity? How?

8. Can our churches find ways of supporting religiously mixed couples?